WEAPONS OF MASS DECEPTION

DEFEAT THE WEAPONS
WORKBOOK

Published by Kudu Publishing

Cover design by: Jeremy Surls
Cover photo by: Julie Watkins   @juliewatkinsphotos

ISBN: 978-1-959095-33-0   2 3 4 5 6 7 8 9 10

Printed in the United States of America

WEAPONS OF MASS DECEPTION

DEFEAT THE WEAPONS
WORKBOOK

ADAM F. JONES

KUDU

CONTENTS

WEAPONS OF
MASS
DECEPTION

THE SILENT STRUGGLE WITHIN
EVERY HIGH PERFORMER

ADAM F. JONES
FORMER U.S. ARMY CAPTAIN AND UH-60 BLACK HAWK PILOT

LIFE-CHANGING LESSONS

"Weapons of mass deception love to draw men
and women away from their assignments, making
them think the noblest thing they can do is sacrifice
their role with their family in order to help others."

READING
TIME

As you read
Chapter 1:
"Life-Changing
Lessons"
in *Weapons
of Mass
Deception*,
review,
reflect on,
and respond
to the text by
answering
the following
questions. If
you have a
group, take
time to share
and discuss
your answers.

REFLECT AND TAKE ACTION:

Have you ever neglected something important in your life due to your ambition in another area? What was it and what did you learn?

_____

_____

_____

_____

_____

_____

_____

_____

_____

_____

_____

_____

When do you think ambition becomes harmful?

_____

_____

_____

_____

_____

_____

_____

_____

_____

When have you been drawn away from your assignment due to influence? Describe the situation.

_____

_____

_____

_____

_____

_____

_____

_____

Have you ever seen the desire for more influence negatively impact another leader? What happened?

_____

_____

_____

_____

_____

_____

_____

_____

Think about an intentional conversation you've had that highlighted the power of communication. What did this conversation do for you?

_____

_____

_____

_____

_____

_____

_____

_____

Do you feel that "the right conversation can change a destiny"? Why or why not?

_____

_____

_____

_____

_____

_____

_____

_____

THE BOTTOM LINE

"What I was suppressing in my heart was spreading into my home. The more that I ignored the war that was waging inside my heart, the worse it got for everyone else."

As you read
Chapter 2:
"The Bottom
Line" in
*Weapons
of Mass
Deception,*
review,
reflect on,
and respond
to the text by
answering
the following
questions. If
you have a
group, take
time to share
and discuss
your answers.

REFLECT AND TAKE ACTION:

What in your life have you attempted to suppress in the past? Did it work, or did it spread? Who has been effected from suppressing and how do you think this makes them feel?

_____

_____

_____

_____

_____

_____

_____

_____

_____

_____

_____

_____

What are you currently pursuing? Why?

_____

_____

_____

_____

_____

_____

_____

What have you pursued in the past? Why?

_____

_____

_____

_____

_____

_____

_____

Of the four weapons of mass deception listed in the BLUF section, which can you most relate to? Explain.

_____

_____

_____

_____

_____

_____

_____

_____

_____

Is your family stressed? Are you adding to it, or taking away from it? What makes you think this?

_____

_____

_____

_____

_____

_____

_____

_____

_____

_____

_____

_____

_____

_____

_____

_____

_____

_____

_____

THE BREAKING POINT

"I was done . . . I had reached my breaking point."

As you read
Chapter 3:
"The Breaking
Point" in
*Weapons
of Mass
Deception*,
review,
reflect on,
and respond
to the text by
answering
the following
questions. If
you have a
group, take
time to share
and discuss
your answers.

REFLECT AND TAKE ACTION:

When have you reached your breaking
point, if ever, in the past? Describe the
situation.

_____

_____

_____

_____

_____

_____

_____

_____

_____

_____

What situation do you think would draw
you closer to your breaking point today?

_____

_____

_____

_____

_____

_____

_____

_____

_____

_____

What do you think will be an indicator of you reaching your breaking point? How will you respond when you detect this indicator early?

_____

_____

_____

_____

_____

_____

Think about a story in your life that mirrors the stories of this section. What did you learn or draw from this experience?

_____

_____

_____

_____

_____

_____

_____

_____

_____

Have you ever struggled with being present? Describe a situation where this has occurred.

_____

_____

_____

_____

_____

_____

_____

_____

_____

_____

_____

_____

_____

_____

_____

_____

_____

_____

_____

_____

_____

WANDERING IN THE WILDERNESS

"The wilderness is not a place of punishment; instead, it's a place of preparation."

As you read Chapter 4: "Wandering in the Wilderness" in *Weapons of Mass Deception*, review, reflect on, and respond to the text by answering the following questions. If you have a group, take time to share and discuss your answers.

REFLECT AND TAKE ACTION:

Do you feel like you are currently "wandering in the wilderness"? What do you think you are meant to do during this time?

_____

_____

_____

_____

_____

_____

_____

_____

_____

Do you believe God is using your time in the wilderness to teach you valuable lessons? Why or why not?

_____

_____

_____

_____

_____

_____

_____

_____

_____

_____

_____

In your own words, what does it mean to reduce your loadout?

_____

_____

_____

_____

_____

_____

_____

How can you reduce your loadout moving forward so you can focus on the things that really matter?

_____

_____

_____

_____

_____

_____

_____

_____

Have you struggled to refine your rhythms? What has blocked you from refining your rhythms in the past?

_____

_____

_____

_____

_____

_____

_____

What are you currently on course for? Is this what you had in mind initially? If not, take time to think on what made you veer off your initial course.

_____

_____

_____

_____

_____

_____

_____

THE WEAPON THAT WAGES WAR

"Weapons of mass deception are the silent killers
hidden in the hearts of most high-performing leaders."

READING TIME

As you read Chapter 5: "The Weapon that Wages War" in *Weapons of Mass Deception*, review, reflect on, and respond to the text by answering the following questions. If you have a group, take time to share and discuss your answers.

REFLECT AND TAKE ACTION:

Are you trying to detect the deception in your life by yourself? Why won't this work?

_____

_____

_____

_____

_____

_____

_____

_____

Are you willing to swallow your pride so those close to you can warn you of the deception that is rooted in your heart? Do you think there is another way to do this by yourself?

_____

_____

_____

_____

_____

_____

_____

_____

_____

In your own words, why is deception so dangerous? What do you feel is the key to defending against deception?

_____

_____

_____

_____

_____

_____

_____

Of the four motives of deception (deter, delay, dissuade, destroy), which do you feel the deception in your life is designed to do?

_____

_____

_____

_____

_____

_____

_____

Do you think you are the only one negatively affected by the deception in your heart, or those around you as well? Does this change your perspective on the need to rid yourself of the deception?

_____

_____

_____

_____

_____

_____

_____

_____

_____

_____

_____

_____

_____

_____

_____

_____

_____

_____

_____

THE HEART, THE HOME, AND THE HEADQUARTERS

"If you want to change your life, start
by changing your heart."

READING TIME

As you read Chapter 6: "The Heart, the Home, and the Headquarters" in *Weapons of Mass Deception*, review, reflect on, and respond to the text by answering the following questions. If you have a group, take time to share and discuss your answers.

REFLECT AND TAKE ACTION:

Of the four causes for weapons of mass deception (transition, training, trauma, timing), where in your heart do you feel the weapons of mass deception formed?

_____

_____

_____

_____

_____

_____

_____

_____

_____

_____

Do you think someone can have more than one weapon of deception in their heart at once? Is this the case with you?

_____

_____

_____

_____

_____

_____

_____

_____

_____

_____

Why is it important to understand the path of weapons of mass deception?

_____

_____

_____

_____

_____

_____

_____

How far along your path is the weapon of mass deception currently in your life? Has it spread from your heart to your home? Has it affected your headquarters?

_____

_____

_____

_____

_____

_____

_____

_____

_____

_____

_____

_____

Why is changing your heart the first step to changing your life?

_____

_____

_____

_____

_____

_____

_____

_____

_____

_____

_____

_____

_____

_____

_____

CHAPTER 7

DRIFT HAPPENS

"Who will you trust to call out the drift in your life?"

REFLECT AND TAKE ACTION:

When have you noticed drift in your
life? What brought your attention to it?

_____

_____

_____

_____

_____

_____

_____

_____

_____

_____

Did you attempt to fix the drift right
away? Why or why not?

_____

_____

_____

_____

_____

_____

_____

_____

_____

_____

_____

_____

If you never fixed the drift that happens in your life, where do you feel you would eventually end up?

_____

_____

_____

_____

_____

_____

_____

_____

Has anyone else ever called out your drift? What did this do for you?

_____

_____

_____

_____

_____

_____

_____

_____

_____

Who do you currently have in your life that can call you out on your drift?

_____

_____

_____

_____

_____

_____

_____

_____

If you were always able to course correct your drift and head in the right direction, where do you feel you would be in 5 years? 10 years?

_____

_____

_____

_____

_____

_____

_____

_____

WEIGHT OF THE WORLD

"Pressure doesn't only bring out some people's best; it can bring out their worst."

READING TIME

As you read Chapter 8: "Weight of the World" in *Weapons of Mass Deception*, review, reflect on, and respond to the text by answering the following questions. If you have a group, take time to share and discuss your answers.

REFLECT AND TAKE ACTION:

What does it mean that "the greatest quality in someone, if left unchecked, can also lead to their destruction"? In your opinion, what is your greatest quality?

_____

_____

_____

_____

_____

_____

_____

_____

_____

_____

In what area(s) of your life do you feel the pressure of performance?

_____

_____

_____

_____

_____

_____

_____

_____

_____

Why do you feel the pressure of performance in this area of your life?

_____

_____

_____

_____

_____

_____

_____

_____

Do you feel your self-worth and worth to others are tied to your performance? Why or why not?

_____

_____

_____

_____

_____

_____

_____

_____

Do you ever seek approval from other people? Do you/have you performed based on your expectation that you will receive approval?

_____

_____

_____

_____

_____

_____

Of the FASTER indicators of the pressure of performance (frustrated, anxious, stressed, tense, exhausted, run-down) which do you feel in your life today?

_____

_____

_____

_____

_____

_____

_____

_____

CHAPTER 9

YOU'RE LEAVING AGAIN?

"I didn't realize my availability did not equal my presence."

REFLECT AND TAKE ACTION:

Can you relate to Captain Brown's story? What part?

_____

_____

_____

_____

_____

_____

_____

_____

_____

_____

In your own words, what is the altar of impact?

_____

_____

_____

_____

_____

_____

_____

_____

_____

_____

_____

In the past, what have you sacrificed on the altar of impact? What was the result of you doing this?

_____

_____

_____

_____

_____

_____

_____

_____

In your current life, what are you sacrificing at the altar of impact? Are you neglecting your role as a father/mother or as a husband/wife to make an impact somewhere else?

_____

_____

_____

_____

_____

_____

_____

_____

Which of the five DRIFT indicators of the altar of impact (disconnected, resentful, irritated, fed up, tense) are you currently experiencing?

_____

_____

_____

_____

_____

_____

_____

Who in your life have you seen drift away from their family due to the altar of impact?

_____

_____

_____

_____

_____

_____

_____

CHAPTER 10

"ONLY A TRUCK DRIVER"

"The cycle of comparison steals our joy. It removes any chance of feeling confident and grateful because we only see what we don't have."

READING TIME

As you read Chapter 10: "'Only a Truck Driver'" in *Weapons of Mass Deception,* **review, reflect on, and respond to the text by answering the following questions. If you have a group, take time to share and discuss your answers.**

REFLECT AND TAKE ACTION:

What stands out to you from the Dr. Sheryl Ziegler "Why Moms are Miserable" excerpt? Is this true for your household?

_____

_____

_____

_____

_____

_____

_____

_____

_____

_____

What areas of your life do you tend to compare to others the most? Your job? Your income?

_____

_____

_____

_____

_____

_____

_____

_____

_____

_____

What is the significance of the word "cycle," in the name of this weapon of mass deception, "The Cycle of Comparison"?

_____

_____

_____

_____

_____

_____

Do you think comparison can ever be healthy? Why or why not?

_____

_____

_____

_____

_____

_____

What do you feel is the difference between comparison and competition?

_____

_____

_____

_____

_____

_____

Of the JUDGED indicators of the cycle of comparison
(jealous, unfulfilled, depleted, greedy, exhausted, distant),
which do you feel present in your life?

_____

_____

_____

_____

_____

_____

How often has your joy been stolen because your default is
to see the gap between your situation and someone else's
success?

_____

_____

_____

_____

_____

WHO HAVE I BECOME?

"If what we do becomes our answer to who
we are, what happens when what we do
is no longer who we want to be?"

As you read
Chapter 11:
"Who Have
I Become?"
in *Weapons
of Mass
Deception,*
review,
reflect on,
and respond
to the text by
answering
the following
questions. If
you have a
group, take
time to share
and discuss
your answers.

REFLECT AND TAKE ACTION:

What is the "Trap of Title"? Have you ever struggled with this trap?

_____

_____

_____

_____

_____

_____

_____

_____

_____

_____

What title or position have you put your identity and significance into in the past? What about today?

_____

_____

_____

_____

_____

_____

_____

_____

_____

_____

Of the DEATH indicators of trap of title (depressed, empty, apathetic, trapped, hollow), which are you currently experiencing in your life?

_____

_____

_____

_____

_____

_____

_____

_____

_____

At what point does your title become a negative in your life?

_____

_____

_____

_____

_____

_____

_____

How can your current title kill your future, greater purpose in life?

_____

_____

_____

_____

_____

_____

_____

_____

_____

_____

_____

_____

_____

_____

_____

_____

_____

_____

_____

BATTLE DAMAGE ASSESSMENT

"Asking someone to help you see where you are drifting or honestly evaluating yourself will be your best way of detecting the weapons."

READING TIME

As you read Chapter 12: "Battle Damage Assessment" in *Weapons of Mass Deception*, review, reflect on, and respond to the text by answering the following questions. If you have a group, take time to share and discuss your answers.

REFLECT AND TAKE ACTION:

Of the four weapons of mass deception discussed (pressure of performance, altar of impact, cycle of comparison, trap of title), which are you currently suffering from?

_____

_____

_____

_____

_____

_____

_____

_____

_____

_____

Take time to take the battle damage assessments provided in the text and write your scores below:

My Pressure of Performance score was _____.

My Altar of Impact score was _____.

My Cycle of Comparison score was _____.

My Trap of Title score was _____.

Which of these four scores is highest? Focus on dismantling this weapon first.

_____

_____

_____

_____

_____

_____

_____

_____

_____

_____

_____

_____

_____

_____

_____

_____

_____

_____

_____

_____

Who in your life can you ask to confirm these scores and conclusions?

_____

_____

_____

_____

_____

_____

_____

_____

_____

_____

_____

_____

_____

_____

_____

_____

_____

_____

_____

TRUST YOUR INSTRUMENTS

"Your feelings might be wrong. We must trust our instruments and the experience of leaders around us."

READING TIME

As you read Chapter 13: "Trust Your Instruments" in *Weapons of Mass Deception*, review, reflect on, and respond to the text by answering the following questions. If you have a group, take time to share and discuss your answers.

REFLECT AND TAKE ACTION:

Why do you think it is so important that leaders trust their "instruments"? What happens when they don't?

_____

_____

_____

_____

_____

Describe the significance of training and order when it comes to dismantling the weapon.

_____

_____

_____

_____

_____

_____

What does it mean that everything is connected? When have you found this to be evident in your life?

_____

_____

_____

_____

_____

_____

What happens if we aren't intentional in this process? Why is this dangerous?

_____

_____

_____

_____

_____

_____

_____

Of the four keys to correction, which do you need to work on most in your current situation and why?

_____

_____

_____

_____

_____

_____

_____

_____

Which of your four primary instruments (peace, people, purpose, power) were you least aware of? How does this instrument keep you on course?

_____

_____

_____

_____

_____

_____

_____

Take time to ask yourself the 4-I questions provided for each of the above instruments to learn more about their significance in your life.

_____

_____

_____

_____

_____

_____

_____

_____

_____

BREAK THE KILL CHAIN

"If you see the attack coming, you can defeat it."

READING TIME

As you read Chapter 14: "Break the Kill Chain" in *Weapons of Mass Deception*, review, reflect on, and respond to the text by answering the following questions. If you have a group, take time to share and discuss your answers.

REFLECT AND TAKE ACTION:

How can awareness be so impactful in defeating the weapons of mass deception?

_____

_____

_____

_____

_____

_____

In your own words, what is a kill chain? What is the kill chain for a weapon of mass deception?

_____

_____

_____

_____

_____

_____

What was the field of formation for the weapon of mass deception you are currently working to dismantle?

_____

_____

_____

_____

_____

_____

What critical experiences have you been through that led to the formation of the weapon of mass deception you are currently working to defeat?

_____

_____

_____

_____

_____

Looking back, what was your subconscious interpretation of the critical experiences you described above?

_____

_____

_____

_____

_____

What automated actions have you taken that led to the formation of the weapon of mass deception that has taken root in your heart?

_____

_____

_____

_____
_____
_____

What have been (or do you think will be) the reinforced results of this weapon of mass deception?

_____
_____
_____
_____
_____

Using the answers you provided above, write down your simplified kill chain below:

• Fields of Formation: _____

• Critical Experiences: _____

• Passive Interpretations: _____

• Automated Actions: _____

• Reinforced Results: _____

CHAPTER 15

SEEING THE SHIFT

"Like most leaders, the pressure of performance is
most likely a weapon that has been causing you
to be unpleasant, easily irritated, and on edge."

READING TIME

As you read Chapter 15: "Seeing the Shift" in *Weapons of MassDeception*, review, reflect on, and respond to the text by answering the following questions. If you have a group, take time to share and discuss your answers.

REFLECT AND TAKE ACTION:

As a leader, is the pressure of performance dictating what you believe to be your value?

_____

_____

_____

_____

_____

_____

_____

_____

_____

_____

Do you believe all leaders experience pressure? What amount of pressure do you believe is normal?

_____

_____

_____

_____

_____

_____

_____

_____

_____

_____

Can you relate to Michael's scenario in this chapter? If so, which parts?

_____

_____

_____

_____

_____

_____

_____

_____

_____

_____

_____

_____

_____

_____

_____

_____

_____

_____

_____

What is your kill chain for Pressure of Performance? Take time to think and write out your answers below:

- Fields of Formation: _____

- Critical Experiences: _____

- Passive Interpretations: _____

- Automated Actions: _____

- Reinforced Results: _____

PRIORITIZING OUR PEOPLE

"We cannot afford to abdicate our ability to impact our children and spouse because we are viewing our responsibilities at home as obligations instead of assignments."

READING TIME

As you read Chapter 16: "Prioritizing Our People" in *Weapons of Mass Deception*, review, reflect on, and respond to the text by answering the following questions. If you have a group, take time to share and discuss your answers.

REFLECT AND TAKE ACTION:

When in your life or the lives of others have you seen a weapon of mass deception manipulate ambition, making it destructive?

_____

_____

_____

_____

_____

_____

_____

_____

_____

_____

_____

What are your priories in life? What comes in second, third, and fourth?

_____

_____

_____

_____

_____

_____

_____

_____

_____

_____

_____

What if God assigned you to your spouse so that you could help them become who they were created to be? Would you be comfortable with this assignment? How would your life change if this were true?

_____

_____

_____

_____

_____

_____

_____

_____

_____

_____

_____

_____

_____

_____

_____

_____

_____

_____

Take time to write your kill chain for the Altar of Impact below:

- Fields of Formation: _____

- Critical Experiences: _____

- Passive Interpretations: _____

- Automated Actions: _____

- Reinforced Results: _____

Of the boundaries given by high-performance leaders toward the end of this chapter, which can you modify and implement into your own life?

_____
_____
_____
_____
_____
_____
_____
_____

OWNING OUR STORY

"To start defeating the cycle of comparison,
we've got to accept responsibility for our story
and then accept that the story isn't over yet."

READING TIME

As you read Chapter 17: "Owning Our Story" in *Weapons of Mass Deception*, review, reflect on, and respond to the text by answering the following questions. If you have a group, take time to share and discuss your answers.

REFLECT AND TAKE ACTION:

When has comparison stolen your joy?

_____

_____

_____

_____

_____

_____

_____

_____

_____

Do you feel social media promotes comparison? Why or why not? How can you defend against this?

_____

_____

_____

_____

_____

_____

_____

_____

_____

_____

_____

_____

What about Katie's scenario in this chapter can you relate to?

_____

_____

_____

_____

_____

_____

_____

_____

Take time to write your kill chain for the Cycle of Comparison:

• Fields of Formation: _____

• Critical Experiences: _____

• Passive Interpretations: _____

• Automated Actions: _____

• Reinforced Results: _____

Do you accept responsibility for your story, or do you blame others for where you are?

_____

_____

_____

_____

_____

_____

_____

_____

Do you recognize that your story is not over? What's stopping you from making the next five, ten, or twenty years the best yet?

_____

_____

_____

_____

_____

_____

_____

_____

_____

BREAKING THE CEILING

"A title doesn't make a person. A person makes the
title. If our title is what gives us a feeling of significance,
then we lose the feeling when we lose the title."

As you read
Chapter 18:
"Breaking
the Ceiling"
in *Weapons
of Mass
Deception*,
review,
reflect on,
and respond
to the text by
answering
the following
questions. If
you have a
group, take
time to share
and discuss
your answers.

REFLECT AND TAKE ACTION:

Have you ever felt limited by the titles you possess?

_____

_____

_____

_____

_____

_____

_____

If you feel you are suffering from Trap of the Title, take the time to listen to a podcast relating to the subject by going to adamfjones.com/podcast. Then, write down what you learned below:

_____

_____

_____

_____

_____

_____

_____

_____

_____

_____

_____

_____

What about Wayne or Elizabeth's scenarios can you relate to?

_____

_____

_____

_____

_____

_____

_____

_____

Take time to write your kill chain for Trap of the Title below:

• Fields of Formation: _____

• Critical Experiences: _____

• Passive Interpretations: _____

• Automated Actions: _____

• Reinforced Results: _____

In your own words, what does it mean that "a title doesn't make a person, a person makes a title"?

_____

_____

_____

_____

_____

_____

_____

_____

_____

_____

_____

_____

_____

_____

_____

_____

_____

_____

_____

_____

MY NEW DECLARATION

"I had to surrender to the goodness of God. I had to trust that His plans for my life were even greater than my ambitions. This is the secret."

ADING TIME

you read Chapter 19: "My New Declaration" in *Weapons of Mass Deception*, review, reflect on, and respond to the text by answering the following questions. If you have a group, take time to share and discuss your answers.

REFLECT AND TAKE ACTION:

Are you willing to put forth the work and make the sacrifices necessary to rid yourself of the weapons of mass deception?

_____
_____
_____
_____
_____
_____
_____
_____
_____
_____

Are you ready to surrender to the Lord fully and trust Him to guide your steps instead of yourself?

_____
_____
_____
_____
_____
_____
_____
_____
_____
_____

APONS OF MASS DECEPTION: WORKBOOK | 79

What needs to happen for you to submit to God fully?

_____
_____
_____
_____
_____
_____
_____
_____
_____
_____
_____
_____
_____
_____
_____
_____
_____
_____
_____
_____

How do you think your life will change if you let God direct your path instead of yourself?

_____

_____

_____

_____

_____

_____

_____

_____

_____

_____

_____

_____

_____

_____

_____

_____

_____

_____

_____

_____

CHAPTER 20

DEPLOY THE TACTICS

"The most important aspect of deploying the counterattack is understanding the compound effect."

As you read
Chapter 20:
"Deploy the
Tactics" in
*Weapons
of Mass
Deception,*
review,
reflect on,
and respond
to the text by
answering
the following
questions. If
you have a
group, take
time to share
and discuss
your answers.

REFLECT AND TAKE ACTION:

The first tactic for deploying the counterattack is silence. How can you make room for silence in your busy life? How can you start with silence, and what do you think this will accomplish?

_____

_____

_____

_____

_____

_____

_____

_____

_____

Who do you need to work on to understand, accept, and appreciate? What's holding you back from doing this today? Who can you talk to in order to better understand and appreciate them?

_____

_____

_____

_____

_____

_____

_____

_____

The third tactic for deploying the counterattack is strategic awareness – what measurement have you been using that has limited your performance and growth? What is a new measurement you can replace this with?

_____

_____

_____

_____

_____

_____

_____

How often do you stop, feel peace, and detach from a situation? How do you think this may be of value?

_____

_____

_____

_____

_____

_____

_____

What healthy trigger response can you implement so you can react appropriately in future situations?

_____

_____

_____

_____

_____

_____

_____

_____

Where can you implement a rhythm of rest and recovery in your life? Can you attach it to an existing activity to make it an easy transition?

_____

_____

_____

_____

_____

_____

_____

What situation or circumstance create stress for you, and what tools or techniques can you introduce to combat this?

_____

_____

_____

_____

_____

_____

_____

In what area of your life can you practice better self-governance? What outlet relieves your stress and encourages self-expression?

_____

_____

_____

_____

_____

_____

_____

Take time to list out three tactics you'll choose to deploy for your counterattack:

- Tactic #1: _____
_____
_____

- Tactic #2: _____
_____
_____

- Tactic #3: _____
_____
_____

CHAPTER 21

BLUE SKY

"Move forward, advance with confidence, and take back any ground that has been stolen from you. Fight for your freedom. Recover all that has been lost."

As you read Chapter 21: "Blue Sky" in *Weapons of Mass Deception*, review, reflect on, and respond to the text by answering the following questions. If you have a group, take time to share and discuss your answers.

REFLECT AND TAKE ACTION:

What do you need to change about the way you are living?

_____

_____

_____

_____

_____

_____

_____

_____

_____

_____

_____

What do you need to change about your environment?

_____

_____

_____

_____

_____

_____

_____

_____

_____

_____

_____

_____

What do you need to change about the way you steward yourself?

_____

_____

_____

_____

_____

_____

_____

What will you implement into your daily routine so once you dismantle the weapons of mass deception, they won't take root again down the road?

_____

_____

_____

_____

_____

_____

_____

Who do you know is struggling with one or more of the weapons of mass deception that you can share this book with?

_____

_____

_____

_____

Once you make it to the "Blue Sky," will you continue to fight forward, push on, and continue your mission? Why or why not?

_____

_____

_____

_____

_____

_____

_____

_____

_____

_____

_____

_____

www.ingramcontent.com/pod-product-compliance
Lightning Source LLC
Chambersburg PA
CBHW062119080426
42734CB00012B/2912